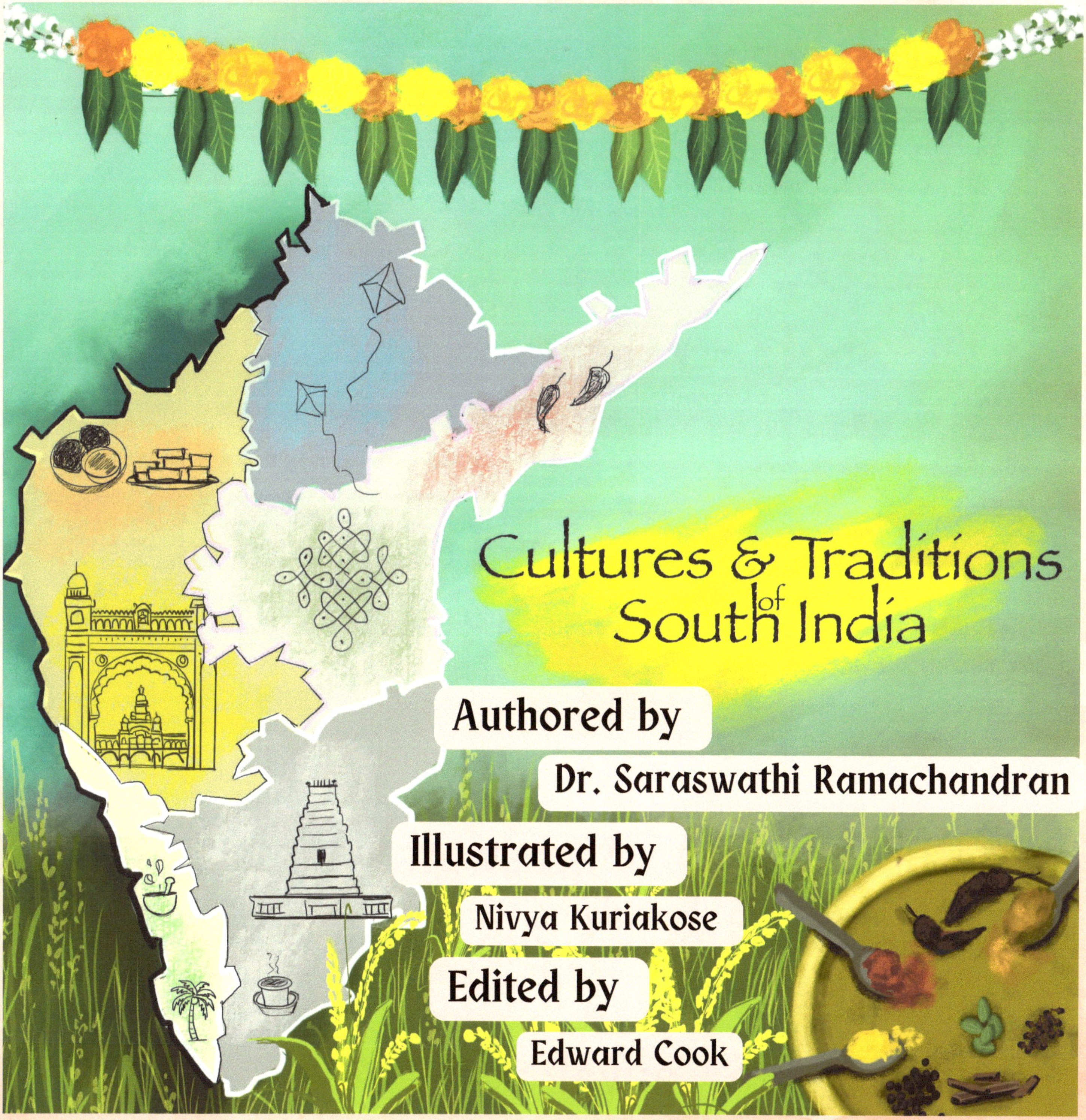

Cultures & Traditions of South India

Authored by

Dr. Saraswathi Ramachandran

Illustrated by

Nivya Kuriakose

Edited by

Edward Cook

Cultures and Traditions of South India

Authored by Dr. Saraswathi Ramachandran
Edited by Edward Cook
llustrated by Nivya Kuriakose
Images from CanvaPro

Copyright and disclaimer

Copyright © 2024 by Dr. Saraswathi Ramachandran
llustrator: Nivya Kuriakose
Editor: Edward Cook
ISBN number: 979-8-9914190-0-0
All rights reserved.

No portion of this book may be reproduced in any form without
written permission from the publisher or author,
except as permitted by the U.S. copyright law.

Disclaimer

Although the author and publisher have made every effort to
ensure that the information in this book was correct at the
time of publication, the author and publisher do not
assume and hereby disclaim any liability to any party
for any loss, damage, or disruption caused by errors
or omissions, whether such errors or omissions result from
negligence, accident, or any other cause.

Introduction

The Indian subcontinent is a large country with a variety of different cultures, languages, cuisines and lifestyles.

There are several states (28) and union territories (8) in the country.

This book gives a brief snapshot of the southern states of India.

The southern states of India include: Kerala, Karnataka, Andhra Pradesh, Telangana and Tamil Nadu.

This book describes some aspects of the culture, cuisine and lifestyles followed in these states.

Several aspects of the culture are practiced across the southern states of India. But they may be called by different names in different regions and may have variations in how they are practiced across these states.

Apart from the major languages, forms of dance, architecture or other features presented in the book, there are other diverse aspects of the culture found in these states.

The material in this book is based on the knowledge gained by the author growing up in South India. It is not a comprehensive report by any means, but just an overview of the beauty of South India, at a glance.

I hope you enjoy this book!

Kerala

Kerala

Kerala, sometimes called 'God's own country', is a beautiful state on the southwestern coast of India.
Famous for coconut trees, beautiful beaches and lush greenery, Kerala also boasts of the amazing Western Ghat mountains.

From spices and festivals, to ancient cultural traditions, Kerala is a unique place for tourism and cultural enrichment.

Famous for Ayurveda, an ancient and powerful holistic system of medicine; Kerala is also a cradle for martial arts, including the incredible dance-fight -'Kalaripayattu'.

Kathakali

Thrissur Pooram

Boat Race

Kalaripayattu

Every year the famous Thrissur Pooram attracts visitors from around the world. The Thrissur Pooram is marked by festivities including decorated elephants, traditional drums and arts and light shows.

The famous snake boat race held every year is another spectacular part of the Kerala tradition.

The language spoken in Kerala is called Malayalam.

The beautiful backwaters of Kerala

The land of coconut trees and boats.

Kathakali performance and snake boat race in Kerala--where nature and culture unite.

'Onam' is an important festival of Kerala and is marked with festivities and tasty delicacies.

'Kathakali' is a famous dance-form from Kerala, which involves story-telling through dance; with vivid makeup and eye expressions.

Tamil Nadu

Tamil Nadu

Tamil Nadu literally means the land of the Tamils. Tamil is a language that is spoken by the people of Tamil Nadu- also known as Tamilians. Tamil is the oldest living language. This means that it is the oldest language which is still actively spoken.

There are various dishes in the Tamil cuisine. An interesting fact about the Tamil and South Indian breakfast is that, in general, it is not sweet. The breakfast dishes are either plain or spicy and include delicious items- such as the Idli, Vada or Dosa, which are served with Sambar and Chutney.

Meenakshi Temple in Madurai

Idlli, Vada, Sambar and Chutney

Nataraja-the Lord of dance

Corridor of the Ramanathaswamy Temple

An excellent classical dance from Tamil Nadu is the BharataNatyam. 'Natyam' means dance. Nataraja is considered to be the cosmic dancer and originator of dance.

The Tamil and South Indian wardrobe consists of the Saree for women and Lungi or Veshti for men.
A Saree is either a 6 yard or a 9 yard long piece of fabric that is draped by women. A veshti, which is also a long piece of white fabric, is used during important occasions by men.

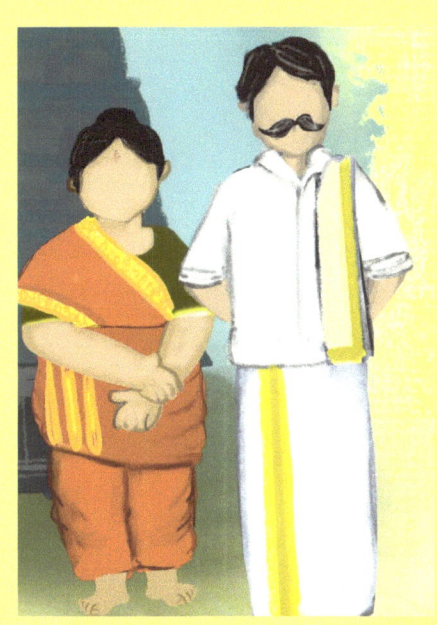

'Pongal', is a harvest festival of the region.

Sri Ranganathaswamy Temple

Madurai Meenakshi temple, decorated with lights.

Thiruvalluvar Statue, near the southernmost tip of the Indian peninsula.

A 'lungi' is a colorful fabric worn by men for casual dressing and daily living.

The Thirukkural is an ancient sacred text written in Tamil. It is renowned for the philosophical messages in it and its greatness as a work of literature. It was written by an eminent Tamil poet and philosopher, Thiruvalluvar.

Tamil Nadu is famous for temples and architectural wonders. The tallest Gopuram (ornate tower at the entrance of a temple), in Asia, at 73 m high, is in Tamil Nadu; at the Sri Ranganatha Swami temple in Srirangam.

Tamil Nadu offers a delectable feast of experiences- from delicious cuisines, to culture and tradition.

Andhra Pradesh

Andhra Pradesh

Andhra Pradesh is the land of the 'Andhras', who speak the language Telugu.

The famous, ancient Tirupati temple in Andhra Pradesh, attracts around 50,000 to 100,000 visitors each day. Pilgrims donate hair at the temple as well. The temple is atop the 7 hills of Tirumala and is a beautiful place to visit.

Vishakhapatnam is a large and beautiful city of beaches in Andhra Pradesh.

'Kuchipudi' is a famous dance-form originating from this place.

Beautiful beach in Visakhapatnam, also called Vizag.

Kites and sweets for the Sankranthi festival.

Mangoes used for making the Avakai pickle.

The Andhra cuisine includes some yummy items such as 'Pesarattu' and 'Avakai': a very spicy side-dish made of raw mangoes pickled with salt and chilli powder.

'Pancha' is the traditional dress for men and is made of a white fabric. Women wear colorful sarees. Half-sarees, also called Langa-onis are popular for young girls and unmarried women.

There are several festivals celebrated. 'Sankranthi' is the harvest festival celebrated in January, when kite-flying is popular.

Dhyana Buddha Statue, in Amaravathi, Andhra Pradesh

Kailasagiri, in Visakhapatnam, Andhra Pradesh

Srikalahasti, temple in Andhra Pradesh

Muggu (called Kolam in Tamil Nadu)- is an artform created in front of the house. This is done early in the morning and often, in the evenings as well.

There are temples and archeological wonders such as the 'Shrikalahasthi' and the 'Dhyana Buddha statue, fascinating traditions and festivals; making Andhra Pradesh uniquely appealing, for tourism and stays.

Telangana

Telangana

The Telangana state is adjacent to Andhra Pradesh and shares the same language as Andhra Pradesh, which is Telugu. Urdu is also spoken here.

There are several famous architectural sites to visit, such as the 'Charminar' (which roughly translates to '4 pillars').

The Golconda fort, an intricately designed complex with a fort and series of caves, was a formidable fortress, and is now a popular tourist attraction.

The Buddha statue in Tank Bund, is the tallest monolith (made of one stone) of Gautama Buddha, and is a beautiful place to visit.

The Charminar, in Hyderabad

Buddha Statue, in the Hussainsagar Lake, Hyderabad

The Ramanuja statue, which is also called the 'Statue of Equality', celebrates the great philosopher, Ramanuja, from the 11th century.

The Ramappa temple, built in the 13th century, is an example of the incredible history and architecture that characterizes India, and is located near Warangal in Telangana.

Ugadi is celebrated, on the Telugu new year day. 'Ugadi pacchadi', is a special mixture with sweet, sour and bitter flavors and represents the various aspects of life: sweet, sour and bitter.

Golconda Fort

Bathukamma Festival Floral arrangement

Biryani

The Bathukamma festival, venerates the Goddess Gowri, with offerings of flowers, shaped up in a mound to resemble a 'gopuram', a structure found at the entrance to temples. This festival celebrates the connection between women, mother earth and nature. It is accompanied by singing and dancing in circles around the floral 'Bathukamma'.

The Statue of Equality- Ramanuja statue

The Ramappa temple in Telangana

Intricately carved figures at the Ramappa temple

Hyderabadi Biryani (a rice dish with a variety of vegetables and spices), is a famous local delicacy.

Yearly festival processions for the Bonalu festival occur in July/August. The Goddess Mahankali is venerated in this traditional 'Jatara' or procession.

The enticing abundance of archaeological and architectural sites, food, culture and celebrations; marks Telangana as another fascinating state, in South India.

Karnataka

Karnataka

Karnataka is a state in South India known for its beautiful natural heritage, beaches, religious sites and rich culture and traditions.

The language spoken in Karnataka is called Kannada.

Karnataka is marked with sites of incredible natural beauty.
These include the long coastline beaches of Mangalore, Udupi and Gokarna.

The Western Ghats or 'Sahyadri' mountains that line the sub-continent on the western side, offer beautiful views and greenery. There are several waterfalls, hiking spots and rich biodiversity, that make the area beautiful and exciting to visit.

MysorePak - a specialty sweet from Karnataka

Murudeshwara Temple

Mysore Palace

Jog falls, Agumbe, Coorg and the Netrani island are some of the famous sites for nature tourism.

Aside from nature tourism, Karnataka also boasts of several intricately designed architectural sites.

These include- the Mysore Palace, the residence of the royal dynasty, in what was once the Kingdom of Mysore. The Dasara parade is held yearly at the palace.

Hampi

Gommateshwara statue in Shravanabelagola, Karnataka

Kotilingeshwara temple

Hampi, which has been declared a World Heritage site by UNESCO, offers a window into the grandiosity and advanced civilization; that represented the Vijayanagara empire in the 12th and 13th centuries.

The Gommateshwara statue is an 18 meter long monolithic statue made of granite. It was created in the 10th century and is an important site for Jain pilgrimage.

The Kotilingeshwara temple has 1 crore (koti) or 10 million lingas. A Shiva Lingam represents Lord Shiva and is a symbol for eternal consciousness.

Gokarna, Karnataka

Udupi Shree Krishna Temple Karnataka

Jog Falls, Karnataka

The Murudeshwara temple, at the shore of the Arabian sea houses the largest statue of Lord Shiva at 37 meters. The temple Gopuram (ornate tower at the entrance to the temple), is the second largest one in India.

The 'Yakshagana' dance is a form of dance-drama found in Karnataka.

All of this, adds to the rich tapestry of art, architecture, culture and splendor of this enchanting tourists' paradise.

Worksheet 1

Match the South Indian state with a feature that characterizes it:

1. Kerala					Pongal

2. Karnataka					Hyderabad

3. Andhra					Kathakali

4. Tamil Nadu					Tirupati

5. Telangana					Kannada

Worksheet 2

Fill in the blanks:

1. Colorful art-form created in front of a South Indian home, especially in the mornings- _____

2. A type of women's attire in South India- _____

3. A type of men's attire in South India- _____

4. Language spoken in Tamil Nadu- _____

5. Language spoken in Kerala- _____

Worksheet 3

Multiple choice questions

1. Which is the oldest living language in the world?

a) Hindu

b) Kalaripayattu

c) Thirukkural

d) Tamil

2. Which state in South India, did the ancient martial arts form, Kalaripayattu, originate in?

a) The Taj Mahal

b) New Delhi

c) Jog falls

d) Kerala

3. Who wrote the Thirukkural?

a) Mahatma Gandhi

b) Mother Theresa

c) Rishi Sunak

d) Thiruvalluvar

4. What is a 'kolam'?

a) A spicy South-Indian breakfast dish

b) A dance-form from South India

c) Traditional attire worn by men in South India

d) An art-form, also called 'muggu' created on the front porch of a home in South India

Glossary

Bharatanatyam: A form of classical dance from South India marked by special expressions, poses, footwork. It connects artistic story-telling, with the spiritual and religious aspects of Hindu mythology.

Biryani: It is a rice dish with various types of vegetables and spices. It can be made as a vegetarian dish or with meat products mixed with the rice.

Bottu: A small circle/dot placed on the forehead, mostly by Hindu Indian women. Usually vermilion or Kumkum is used to make the dot. Readymade stickers are also often used. The peel-off stickers and Bottu designs can range from a simple dot, to elaborate decorative patterns.

Idli: a breakfast dish made of steamed rice and lentils that are ground, mixed and fermented overnight.

Kathakali: A dance form from Kathakali involving elaborate costumes and facial expressions. The themes involve stories from Hindu mythology or the ancient sacred texts.

Kolam/muggu: an art-form drawn in front of the house, often with rice flour or chalk, especially in the mornings or evenings. The intricate designs are also often colored in. Kolams represent the welcoming of auspiciousness and prosperity into the house.

Kuchipudi: It is a classical dance-form from South India originating from Andhra Pradesh. It involves the re-telling of mythological stories and incorporates distinct costumes, poses and hand gestures.

References and further reading:

1. https://www.keralatourism.org/

2. https://www.karnatakaecotourism.com/

3. https://tourism.ap.gov.in/home

4. https://tourism.telangana.gov.in/

5. https://www.tamilnadutourism.tn.gov.in/

6. https://www.hinduamerican.org/blog/nataraja-cosmic-dancer-symbolism

Authored by Dr. Saraswathi Ramachandran, Ilustrated by Nivya Kuriakose (images from CanvaPro) and edited by Edward Cook. This book is an attempt at a brief description of the rich culture and lifetyles found in South india.